Fact Finders

ENDANGERED
RIVERS

INVESTIGATING RIVERS IN CRISIS

Rani Iyer

raintree

a Capstone company — publishers for children

Raintree is an imprint of Capstone Global Library Limited, a company incorporated in England and Wales having its registered office at 264 Banbury Road, Oxford, OX2 7DY – Registered company number: 6695582

www.raintree.co.uk
myorders@raintree.co.uk

Editor: Abby Colich
Designer: Bobbie Nuytten
Media researcher: Gina Kammer
Original illustrations © Capstone Global Library Limited 2020
Production Specialist: Tori Abraham
Originated by Capstone Global Library Ltd

ISBN 978 1 4747 9243 1 (hardback)
ISBN 978 1 4747 9251 6 (paperback)

British Library Cataloguing in Publication Data
A full catalogue record for this book is available from the British Library.

Acknowledgements
We would like to thank the following for permission to use photographs: Corbis: Bettmann, 13, Bob Sacha, 17, JAI/Jane Sweeney, 27; Dreamstime: Mikhail Blajenov (top), 23; Getty Images: Dorling Kindersley, 6; Newscom: EPA/Khaled El-Fiqi, 21, Ingram Publishing, (bottom), 23, Reuters/Brazil/Stringer, 20, Reuters/Nir Elias, 25; North Wind Picture Archives: 8; Shutterstock: alexmisu (top left), cover, Arseniy Krasnevsky (back), cover, 1, Asianet-Pakistan, 9, Baloncici, 18, Colin Stitt (top right), cover, cubephoto, 24, Geoffrey Kuchera, 29, guentermanaus, 5, irisphoto1, 19, joppo, 12, Kekyalyaynen, 26, KPG Ivary, 28, Luciano Queiroz, 7, niall dunne, 4, Oliver Sved (bottom left), cover, Ruud Morijn Photographer, 22, Sasilssolutions, 14, Strahil Dimitrov, 15, Vadym Zaitsev, 16, wk1003mike, 10, WvdM (bottom right), cover, Zorandim, 11.

We would like to thank our content consultant, Dr Thomas M. Neeson, Postdoctoral Researcher from the Department of Limnology at the University of Wisconsin–Madison, USA, for his invaluable help in the preparation of this book.

Every effort has been made to contact copyright holders of material reproduced in this book. Any omissions will be rectified in subsequent printings if notice is given to the publisher.

Printed and bound in the United Kingdom.

Contents

CHAPTER 1
A world of rivers

Rivers, streams and creeks flow on every continent on Earth.

Water rushes over rocks and down a waterfall. Beavers build dams with tree branches. A bird swoops down and grabs a fish with its bill. Crayfish munch on algae. All sorts of creatures live in or near rivers. People depend on rivers for survival too. Much of our drinking water comes from rivers and streams. Rivers are an important part of Earth's landscape.

As much as humans rely on rivers, we have caused great harm to this resource. Human actions have **endangered** rivers. Several rivers are drying up. Others are severely **polluted**. Some fish **species** that once thrived are now nearly **extinct**. Experts believe that the world will suffer a major water crisis if rivers are not cleaned up and protected.

endanger to put at risk

pollute to make something dirty or unsafe

species group of plants or animals that share common characteristics

extinct no longer living; an extinct species is one that has died out, with no more of its kind

Rivers around the world are becoming littered with rubbish.

Parts of a river

source — the place where a river begins, usually a spring, glacier or lake

tributary — a creek, stream, brook or other river that flows into a larger river

channel — the course a river takes through land

meander — a bend or turn in a river's channel

bank — the land alongside a river

floodplain — area of land next to a river where water can overflow

delta — area of land that forms at the mouth of a river

mouth — where a river ends, usually into another river or the sea

What is a river?

A river is a body of **fresh** water. Its **current** flows in one direction. Rivers usually start in high places. They flow downhill and empty into another body of water.

No two rivers are alike. The shape and course of a river changes over time. Some rivers, such as the Rhine in Europe, are deep and wide and flow slowly. Other rivers, such as the Trinity River in California, USA, rush quickly, creating rapids and waterfalls. Some rivers flow only during seasons of heavy rain. Occasionally some rivers flow partly underground.

current movement of water in a river or an ocean

ecosystem group of animals and plants that interact with their surroundings

invertebrate animal without a backbone

food web many food chains connected to one another

Life in a river

Rivers and the organisms they support form a complex **ecosystem**. A perfect place for life to thrive, rivers are home to almost every kind of organism. Trees and other plants grow in the river and along its banks. Insects and other **invertebrates** float on the surface and crawl on the riverbed below. Rivers are filled with fish. Frogs, turtles, snakes and otters also call rivers home. Life too small to see, such as phytoplankton, is an important part of river **food webs**.

Fish are just one type of the many organisms in a river's ecosystem.

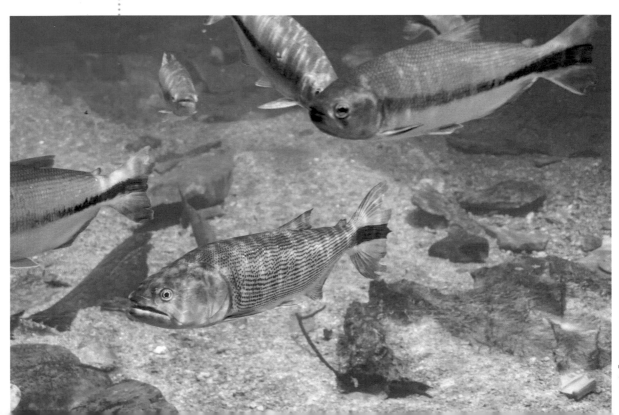

Rivers and people

People have settled near rivers throughout history. Ancient peoples built cities along riverbanks. They used river water to grow crops. They fished and built boats to travel in. They travelled down rivers to trade for goods.

People continue to use rivers in the same way today. Rivers provide water that is used for drinking, bathing, cooking and cleaning. Freshwater fish are an important part of the diets of millions of people. Ferries carry people over rivers from one place to another. Millions of tons of goods travel down rivers every day.

In past times, people used rivers to transport goods from place to place. This was quicker than using roads, which weren't very good or didn't yet exist.

The water in the air, rivers, lakes and underground stores accounts for 1 per cent of all water on Earth. This 1 per cent must provide fresh water for everyone on Earth. The rest of Earth's water is in the oceans and frozen in polar ice caps.

Humans have newer uses for rivers too. River water can generate **hydroelectric** power. Some kinds of fish and prawns are farmed in rivers. Rivers support sports and recreational activities.

hydroelectric to do with the production of electricity from moving water

Life on the Indus River in Sukkur, Pakistan

CHAPTER 2
Pollution and rivers

From drinking water to food, rivers provide for many human needs. But humans have also severely damaged rivers. Scientists say half of the world's major rivers are seriously polluted. Pollution comes from many different places. It can come from farms, industries and people. It is a constant threat to life within rivers.

Pollution from farming

Farming is the leading cause of pollution in many areas today. Most farmers choose to use fertilizers and pesticides to help grow their crops. Many fertilizers and pesticides contain chemicals that are toxic. When crops are watered or rain falls, the chemicals wash off with the water. The **run-off** flows into nearby rivers.

Large numbers of dead fish are now appearing more frequently in rivers due to pollution.

These chemicals damage rivers in many ways. The chemicals from fertilizers help plants grow. But in a river they can cause extra algae to grow. When the algae dies, it takes oxygen away from other organisms. The chemicals in pesticides kill pests that harm crops. If they end up in a river, they can kill fish, birds and other creatures.

In addition to chemicals, animal waste also flows from farms into rivers. This causes a loss in the amount of oxygen in a river. Animals that live in the river can die as a result.

run-off water that flows over land instead of soaking into the ground

This farmer is treating his wheat crop with a chemical pesticide.

Industrial pollution

Industrial pollution is any waste that comes from an industry or business. Since the 19th century, factories that make items such as clothing, paper and medicine have dumped their liquid waste into rivers. This waste contains substances that are toxic. Sometimes these toxins kill fish and other animals straight away. They can also enter the **food chain** when small fish eat plants. Bigger fish build up toxins in their bodies when they eat smaller fish. These bigger fish can in turn be toxic to humans who eat them. Sometimes companies dump liquid waste into rivers that is much hotter than the water temperature. River life that cannot handle the rise in temperature is threatened.

food chain series of organisms in which each one in the series eats the one preceding it

Industrial waste flowing into a river

Cuyahoga River fire

An incident several decades ago in the United States led to major improvements for rivers there. In 1969, pollution caused part of the Cuyahoga River in the state of Ohio to catch fire. The fire was small, but people were angry. This was not the first time the river had caught fire. The first fire was in 1936. The river caught fire several more times, including a very large fire in 1952. But the response to the 1969 fire led to the creation of new laws in 1972. These laws placed limits on what companies could dump into water.

Over the past few decades, governments have passed laws that have helped reduce the amount of waste companies can dump into water. But that doesn't stop some companies from illegally dumping their waste. The laws are not easy to enforce. In some places there are no laws that prevent this pollution. Industrial waste remains a threat to the world's rivers.

. . . Cuyahoga River fire of 1952

Sewage

Where does the water from toilets, baths and sinks go? Human waste, soaps, cleaners and everything else that goes down the drain often ends up in rivers. In some areas, sewage is cleaned in a treatment plant. The treated water is then dumped into rivers. But not all toxins can be removed during treatment. Many harmful pollutants still enter the water. Over time these can poison life that depends on the river water, including humans. There are many areas all over the world where sewage is not treated or cleaned before it is dumped into rivers. People who swim or bathe in the water can become ill. Wildlife is poisoned.

... This sewage drain is releasing dirty water.

.... Rubbish illegally dumped near a river

Litter and dumping

Litter, or any kind of solid rubbish, might be the most obvious kind of river pollution. Some people carelessly throw rubbish in rivers. At other times, litter is carried by wind or storm drains. All this dirties the water and harms river life. Fish or birds swallow bits of rubbish that they think is food. This damages the animals' bodies and sometimes kills them. Sometimes they can get caught or tangled in rubbish and become trapped. When rubbish such as plastic breaks down, it releases toxins that poison the water. These toxins are harmful to the life that depends on the water.

From air to water

Pollution from the air also harms rivers. Carbon dioxide is a gas that occurs naturally in the air. This gas is also released into the air when people use certain fuels such as petrol. Over time, too much carbon dioxide has collected in the air. Carbon dioxide naturally helps trap heat on the Earth. But too much carbon dioxide is causing the Earth to become warmer. If the Earth becomes too warm, the environment is at risk.

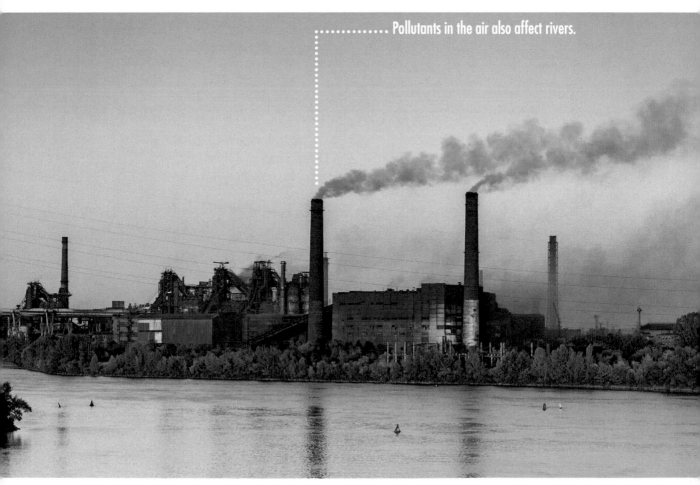

Pollutants in the air also affect rivers.

Warmer temperatures are causing some rivers to dry up. In some areas, changes in climate are causing less **precipitation**. Less rain and snow means less water for rivers. Also, when water warms up, it **evaporates** more quickly, causing rivers to dry up. River life cannot thrive without enough water.

While some rivers are drying up, others are flooding more often. Warmer temperatures cause snow and ice to melt. Some areas are receiving more rain and snow than what is normal. These factors lead to more flooding. It is normal for rivers to flood sometimes. But an increase in flooding is harmful to rivers and the humans who live near them. When floodwater **recedes**, oil, petrol, chemicals from farms and rubbish go with it. The water fills with toxins that are harmful to life in and near the water.

precipitation falling of water from the sky in the form of rain, sleet, hail or snow

evaporate to change from liquid into gas

recede to move back and away

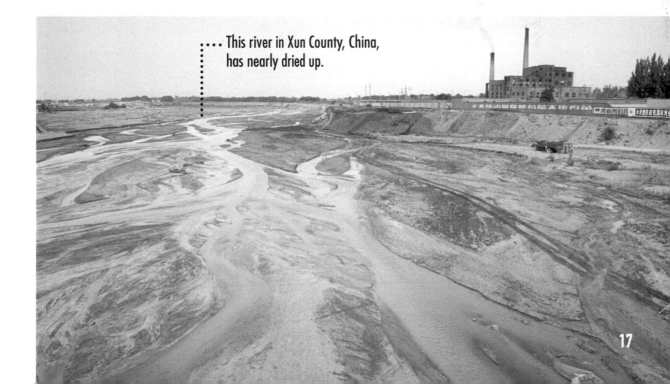

This river in Xun County, China, has nearly dried up.

17

Flooding has destroyed this road.

CHAPTER 3

More damage

Pollution is not the only thing harming the world's rivers. Development, fishing, overuse and **invasive species** all play a part in harming river water and the life that depends on it.

Development along rivers

Throughout history, people have settled near rivers. But, over time, people began building bigger structures closer to rivers. This caused pollution to enter rivers more easily. Building has caused floodplain areas to develop. When rivers flood, the water has nowhere else to go. Water fills the floodplain. When water recedes, pollution and rubbish travels with it.

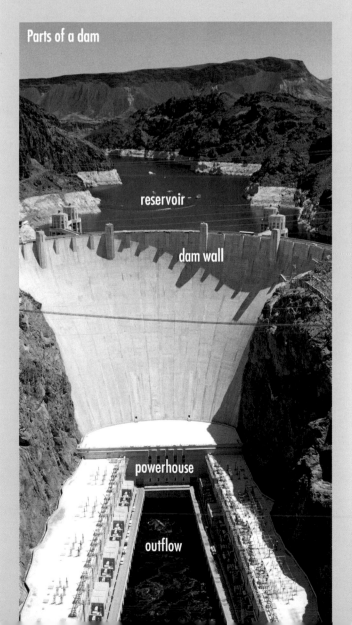

Parts of a dam

reservoir

dam wall

powerhouse

outflow

Dams

Dams are structures built to stop the flow of river water. The water is collected and held in a reservoir. Dams have many benefits. They supply water for crops, create hydroelectric power and provide drinking water. But dams disrupt the natural flow of rivers. When dams block their environment, fish cannot move to **breed** or find food. Dams also trap **sediment**. Areas downstream need sediment. Lack of sediment causes erosion. Too much **erosion** can kill plants and trees that grow along a riverbank.

invasive species plants or animals that have been artificially introduced into an ecosystem

breed to mate and produce young

sediment bits of sand or clay carried by water or wind

erosion wearing away of land by water or wind

Overfishing

In many countries, people rely on freshwater fish as a main source of protein. Without limits on the amount fishers can catch, the number of fish has declined. When one species runs low, fishers begin catching another. If this trend continues, scientists believe the world's rivers will reach dangerously low levels of fish. Several species of river fish are now endangered due to overfishing. These include the arapaima in the Amazon River, the Murray cod in Australia and the sockeye salmon in the United States.

... Fishing of the arapaima is now allowed only once a year in Brazil.

.... Fish farm in the Nile River in Egypt

Overuse

People have always depended on rivers for their survival. As the human population has grown, so has the impact on rivers. Rivers are used for farming, industry and drinking water. Experts say that if this pressure on rivers continues, some rivers may dry up before they reach the sea. One place where this is particularly true is China. Parts of the Yellow River have dried up due to overuse.

People must find ways to reduce the amount of water used from rivers. Continued overuse of river water will impact people and wildlife in many negative ways.

Fish farms

Pollution is killing many fish. Too much fishing is also leading to a decline in the number of wild fish. People are now creating fish farms in some rivers. Fish farms can help increase food supplies. Cages of carp, tilapia, salmon and catfish are raised on farms in some rivers. But fish farms can harm rivers. Food for the fish can cause the growth of too much algae. Also, when so many fish live too close together, they can become diseased. Diseases can spread to other life in the river, including wild fish.

Invasive species

Invasive species are plants and animals that move from their habitat into a new one. Sometimes they arrive in a new habitat accidentally. They may be carried by boat. But humans also introduce them to a new area on purpose. Invasive species multiply and eventually harm a local ecosystem. They also prey on local species. Other invasive species take resources and habitats away from local species. Local species can decline to the point of becoming endangered. Invasive species often have no predators in their new environment. They continue to reproduce and take over the new area.

Non-native invasive species are considered the second greatest threat to native wildlife in the UK and cost the UK economy up to £1.7 billion per year. These species include Japanese knotweed, floating pennywort, giant hogweed and Himalayan balsam. All these species threaten ecosystems in rivers.

...... Giant hogweed

River life at risk

All over the world, river life is affected by the harm humans have caused to rivers. Many river species are now endangered.

The Mekong catfish is found in Asia's Mekong River. This giant catfish weighs about 300 kilograms (660 pounds). Overfishing and damming have led to this fish's decline.

The river terrapin was once abundant in parts of Asia. But this turtle, along with its eggs, are hunted for food.

The population of the Southern River Otter, native to South America, has declined in recent years. Habitat destruction and illegal hunting are to blame.

The green pitcher plant was once common along rivers in the south-eastern United States. There are only a handful of these insect-eating plants remaining in the wild. Development as well as collection for commercial trade have led to its decline.

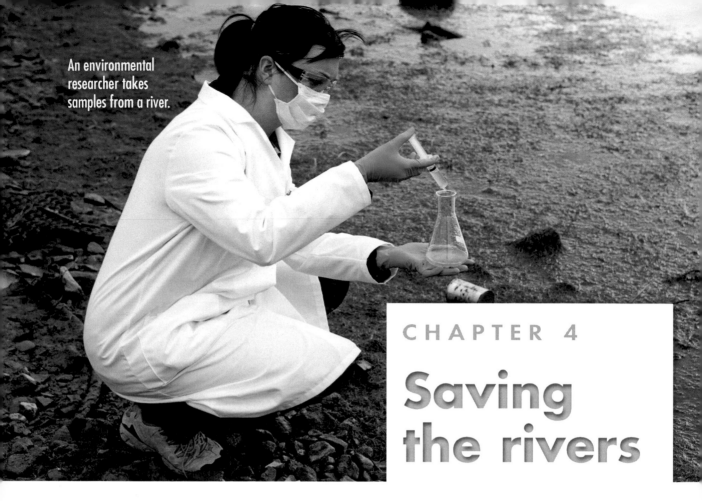

An environmental researcher takes samples from a river.

CHAPTER 4

Saving the rivers

The world's rivers are drying up, flooding more often and full of pollution. Some species are declining. Ecosystems are changing. But people still depend on rivers for survival. This vital resource must be cleaned up and protected. What needs to happen to save the world's rivers?

Better laws

In the UK, the 2003 Water Act makes it a crime to cause or allow polluting or poisonous waste to be put in waters without permission. In June 2019, the Canal & River Trust of England and Wales stated that plastic makes up 59 per cent of waste in Britain's inland waters.

Drinking water from the sea

Some areas are turning to the sea for their drinking water as rivers dry up. Factories that take salt out of seawater are now found throughout the world. After the salt is removed, the water is supplied to cities. However, the process requires a lot of energy. Using this extra energy releases more carbon dioxide into the air.

More laws to protect fresh water are needed around the world. Many rivers run through more than one country. Polluted water from one country flows into another. The United Nations is one organization working to protect the world's water. It launched the "Water for Life" decade in 2005. Countries must work together to create laws to protect the world's water.

Salt is extracted from seawater at this plant on the Mediterranean Sea in Hadera, Israel

Slow down development

Many people live along riverbanks. Some businesses thrive near rivers. People depend on dams for many uses. Governments are removing some dams to improve the health of rivers. But it's not practical to tear down all development near rivers. People and governments must work together to stop more development along rivers. Less development will prevent further pollution and protect river life.

Better farming

If land can be better protected from pollution, then rivers will benefit too. Less toxic pesticides and fertilizers must be developed and used. Ways to prevent toxic run-off must also be developed. If the world changes the way it farms, a leading cause of river pollution will end.

Better sewage treatment

Pollution from sewage is a problem for many rivers. Even sewage that has been treated and cleaned can still poison river life. Scientists must work to develop better water treatment systems. People must be educated about what is safe to flush down the toilet. Governments must make the necessary updates to sewage systems.

These storage tanks prevent waste water from being released into a river.

River success

With careful planning, it is possible to improve the condition of some rivers. In the 1950s, a motorway was built on top of the Cheonggyecheon, a stream in Seoul, South Korea. A project to restore the 11-kilometre (7-mile) long stream was launched in 2003. Officials decided to tear down the motorway and let the water flow free again. Native trees were planted along the riverbanks. Soon fish, birds and animals began returning to the water.

Better energy

Some people are pushing the world to use cleaner energy. This energy produces little or no carbon dioxide. Less extra carbon dioxide in the air will help prevent higher temperatures on Earth. This will slow climate change and its negative effects on rivers.

The Cheonggyecheon stream in Seoul, South Korea

People doing their bit

It will take a global effort to clean up the world's rivers. But everyone can make changes at home that will help keep rivers clean.

Save water

Make sure that washing machines and dishwashers are full before starting. Turn off the sink when brushing teeth. Take shorter showers. Taking a short shower instead of filling up a bath can save 42 litres (11 gallons) of water.

Be mindful of what is flushed

Water treatment plants can't remove everything. By not flushing harmful substances such as medicine down the toilet, river life can be spared from being exposed to some toxins.

Use less electricity and fuels

When fossil fuels are used, carbon dioxide is released into the air. The more carbon dioxide is in the air, the warmer the Earth is going to get. More damage to the planet, including rivers, is going to occur.

Volunteer with a local river or stream clean-up programme

Volunteer to help plant native tree species near riverbanks. Tree roots hold soil in place and help control floodwaters during the rainy times.

Keep water clean

Throw rubbish away in its proper place. Don't litter. It may end up in a river. Don't dump anything down a drain. Anything dumped will probably end up in a river.

A lot of change must happen. There's a lot of work to do to clean up the world's rivers. The people of the world must unite to prevent more damage. Rivers are a resource definitely worth saving and protecting.

Glossary

breed to mate and produce young

current movement of water in a river or an ocean

ecosystem group of animals and plants that interact with their surroundings

endanger to put at risk

erosion wearing away of land by water or wind

evaporate to change from liquid into gas

extinct no longer living; an extinct species is one that has died out, with no more of its kind

food chain series of organisms in which each one in the series eats the one preceding it

food web many food chains connected to one another

hydroelectric to do with the production of electricity from moving water

invasive species plants or animals that have been artificially introduced into an ecosystem

invertebrate animal without a backbone

pollute to make something dirty or unsafe

precipitation falling of water from the sky in the form of rain, sleet, hail or snow

recede to move back and away

run-off water that flows over land instead of soaking into the ground

sediment bits of sand or clay carried by water or wind

species group of plants or animals that share common characteristics

Comprehension questions

1. How have humans damaged the world's rivers? Use evidence from the text to support your answers.

2. Look at the photos on pages 8 and 9. Based on what you've read in the text, how do you think human interactions with rivers have changed over time? How have they stayed the same?

3. How might the world be different if clean and renewable energy sources were more commonly used than fossil fuels. Use evidence from the text and other print and reliable internet sources to support your answer.

Find out more

Are Humans Damaging the Atmosphere? (Earth Debates), Catherine Chambers (Raintree, 2016)

Protecting Our Planet (Beyond the Headlines), Jilly Hunt (Raintree, 2018)

Rivers (Where on Earth?), Susie Brooks (Wayland, 2017)

Rivers and Coasts (Geographics), Izzi Howell (Franklin Watts, 2018)

Science vs Climate Change (Science Fights Back), Nick Hunter (Raintree, 2017)

Sustainable Energy (Let's Think About), Vic Parker (Raintree, 2015)

The Great Debate: The Future of Energy (Engage Literacy), Melanie Waldron (Raintree, 2017)

Websites

Visit this website for a simple explanation of the greenhouse effect: **climatekids.nasa.gov/greenhouse-effect/**

Visit this CBBC website for information about greenhouse gases, global warming and the ozone layer, and what you can do to help the planet:

news.bbc.co.uk/cbbcnews/hi/find_out/guides/world/global_warming/newsid_1575000/1575441.stm

Index